D1315463

PRIMARY SOURCES OF EVERYDAY LIFE IN COLONIAL AMERICA™

Inventors and Inventions in Colonial America

Charlie Samuel

The Rosen Publishing Group's
PowerKids Press™
New York

Published in 2003 by The Rosen Publishing Group, Inc.
29 East 21st Street, New York, NY 10010

First Edition

Photo Credits: Key: t: top, b: bottom, c: center, l: left, r: right
p.4tl Mary Evans Picture Library; p.4b Peter Newark's American Pictures; p.7tl Corbis/
Roman Soumar; p.7b Corbis/Historical Picture Archive; p.8tl Corbis/Philadelphia
Museum; pp. 8br, 11tr Peter Newark's Amercian Pictures; p.11b Corbis/Library of
Congress; p.12tl Bridgeman Art Library/Company of Philadelphia; p.12br, 15tr Peter
Newark's American Pictures; p.15b Art Archive/New York Public Library; p.16tl Peter
Newark's American Pictures; p.16b Getty Images/Cameron Davidson; p.19, 20b Peter
Newark's American Pictures.

Library of Congress Cataloging-in-Publication Data
Samuel, Charlie.
  Inventors and inventions in colonial America / Charlie Samuel.
     p. cm. — (Primary sources of everyday life in colonial America)
Includes bibliographical references and index.
  ISBN 0-8239-6601-1
 1. Inventors—United States—History—17th century—Biography—Juvenile literature.
2. Inventors—United States—History—18th century—Biography—Juvenile literature. 3.
Inventions—United States—History—17th century—Juvenile literature. 4. Inventions—
United States—History—18th century—Juvenile literature. 5. United States—Social life
and customs—To 1775—Juvenile literature. I. Title. II. Series.
  T39 .S25 2003
  609.74'09032—dc21
                                                                          2002004836

Contents

1. Colonies in North America 5

2. Building on Ideas from Europe 6

3. Benjamin Franklin: A Leading Colonial
   Scientist 9

4. Benjamin Franklin: A Man of Many Inventions 10

5. David Rittenhouse and the First Telescope
   in the Colonies 13

6. Sybilla Masters: The First American
   Woman Inventor 14

7. Benjamin Banneker: The First African
   American Scientist 17

8. Thomas Jefferson: Statesman and
   Inventor 18

9. Wagons and Weapons 21

10. Remembering America's Early Inventors 22

Glossary 23

Index 24

Primary Sources.................................... 24

Web Sites.. 24

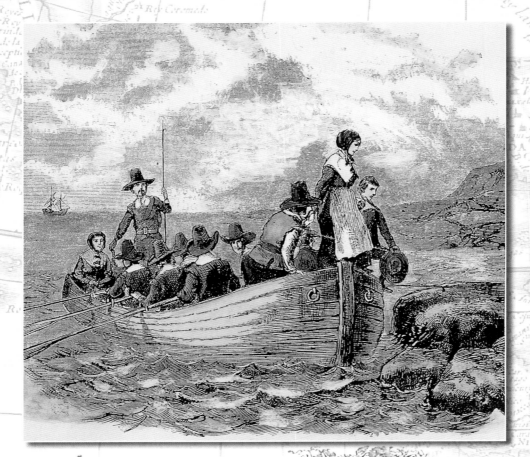

◀ The Pilgrims, a group of English colonists, landed at Plymouth Rock, Massachusetts, in 1620. They hoped to find a home where they could worship as they wished.

▼ Thomas West, Lord De La Warre, gives thanks for his group's safe arrival in America. West was the first governor of Virginia.

Colonies in North America

Europeans first heard about America at the end of the fifteenth century. Soon, European settlers began communities, called **colonies**, in America. The first colonies were started by the Spanish in the areas that are now known as Mexico and southwestern United States. The French started a colony in present-day Canada. Later, France also claimed Louisiana, which was a huge area west of the Mississippi River. The Dutch and the Swedish also had small colonies. Most colonies, however, belonged to England. By 1669, thirteen English colonies stretched, along the East Coast, from New England to Georgia.

The Europeans' new home was also home to many Native American peoples. Europeans thought that Native Americans knew little about science. In fact, friendly Native Americans taught the newcomers new ways of farming and how to make medicine from plants. Without such help, many of the first colonists would have died from either starvation or sickness.

Building on Ideas from Europe

Colonial inventors were interested in the kinds of sciences that helped them in their daily lives. Those sciences included **agriculture**, or farming, medicine, and botany, the study of plants. **Astronomy** was also important. Studying the stars and the planets allowed people to measure the changing seasons. Another important science was **surveying**. Surveyors measured land. They mapped the places where one farm ended and another began, or even the places where one colony ended and another began.

The early colonists used European tools and machines. They got fields ready for planting by using a plow to turn the soil, for example. The plow was pulled by horses or oxen. Colonists used windmills and water mills to grind grain into flour between turning stones. Windmills used the wind to turn the grindstones. Water mills used the power of water from a stream. Milling was very important. By 1650, Virginia had four windmills and five water mills.

◄ This windmill was built in Nantucket in 1746. The top of the building turns so that the sails always face the wind.

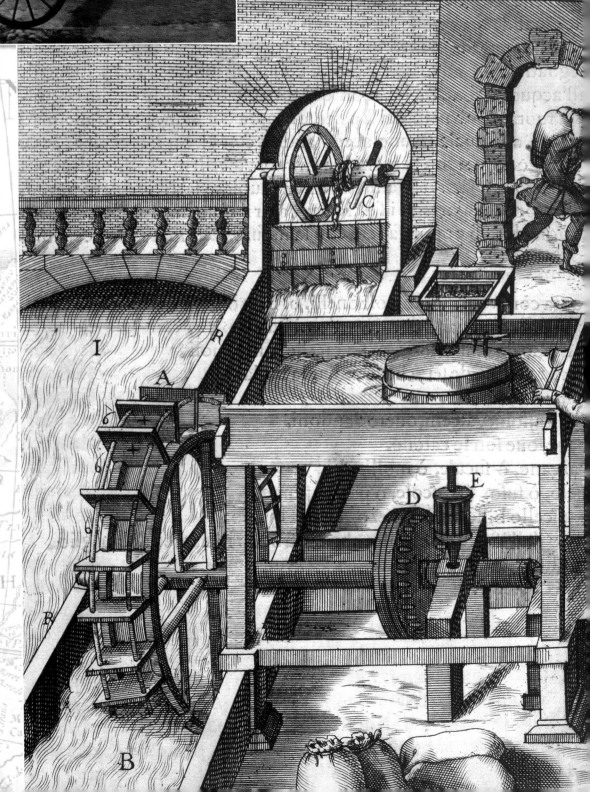

► This is a diagram of a water mill in the early 1600s. Running water turned the large wheel, which then turned the stones that ground the grain into flour. The flour was collected in sacks.

This picture shows Benjamin Franklin as a great hero who is trying to catch electricity from lightning during a storm. In reality, being struck by lightning would have badly hurt Franklin or might even have killed him. However, his ideas and experiments were important in the study of electricity.

When Franklin arrived in Philadelphia in 1723 he was very poor. Some say he only had a loaf of bread to eat. His printing business and his inventions helped him to become very wealthy.

Benjamin Franklin: A Leading Colonial Scientist

Benjamin Franklin was one of the most famous people in eighteenth-century America. He was a scientist, but he also printed a newspaper, wrote books, and helped to write the U.S. **Constitution** in 1787.

Franklin was born in 1706, in Boston, Massachusetts. At age 12, he became an **apprentice** and learned to use a **printing press**. Later, Franklin started a newspaper in Philadelphia, Pennsylvania. In 1743, he formed the American Philosophical Society to discuss useful ways to help Philadelphia, such as having lights along the streets or a paid police force. Franklin also founded the Philadelphia Academy to train people in the arts and the sciences.

From 1748 to 1790, Franklin was a politician. He helped to lead the colonies to independence from English rule in the American Revolution, which began in 1775.

Benjamin Franklin: A Man of Many Inventions

Benjamin Franklin was interested in how science could improve life. He worked out a way to create electricity, but not how to use electricity to provide light or heat. Franklin is said to have once flown a kite during a storm. In the story, he tied an iron key to the string of the kite. The key gathered electricity from the storm clouds. This told Franklin that lightning must be a kind of electricity that built up in clouds during a storm.

Franklin invented the lightning rod, which stopped wooden buildings from being set on fire by lightning. The rod carried electricity straight to the ground.

Among Franklin's other inventions was an iron stove that created more heat than an open fire. He also invented bifocals, eyeglasses that helped people with poor eyesight to see better. He invented a device that could measure how far a carriage had traveled, and also a way to make ships more watertight and therefore safer.

▶ This picture shows Franklin flying his kite in a thunderstorm. Franklin realized that lightning was actually a form of electricity.

▼ These people are using a machine based on Franklin's inventions related to electricity. People thought it was fun to create small electric shocks.

◄ This engraving shows David Rittenhouse with his telescope. Using the telescope, he made discoveries about the planet Venus.

► This image shows Benjamin Franklin at his newspaper press in Philadelphia. Franklin was a good friend of David Rittenhouse. Both men belonged to the American Philosophical Society, which met to talk about ideas and ways of improving life in America.

David Rittenhouse and the First Telescope in the Colonies

David Rittenhouse was born in 1732, in Germantown, Pennsylvania. When he grew up, he became a clockmaker, surveyor, and inventor.

Telescopes were already in use in Europe, but David Rittenhouse built the first telescope in America. The lenses of the telescope made faraway objects seem closer. Using his telescope, Rittenhouse discovered that the planet Venus has an atmosphere, or a layer of gas around it.

Rittenhouse was also a famous surveyor. He made fine machines, such as **compasses**, to use in surveying. He helped to set Pennsylvania's borders with its neighboring colonies, which included Maryland, New Jersey, Massachusetts, and New York. In 1768, Rittenhouse became a member of Benjamin Franklin's American Philosophical Society.

Rittenhouse later became an important official in Pennsylvania and then in the United States, after it was created in 1776.

Sybilla Masters: The First American Woman Inventor

No one knows much about the early life of Sybilla Masters. By 1712, however, she had married a merchant named Thomas Masters and was living in Philadelphia, Pennsylvania.

Sybilla Masters came up with a new way to make cornmeal. Indian corn was usually ground into flour using wheels. Masters invented a machine that broke up the corn with hammers. It made a **hominy meal**, which Masters used to make grits.

In 1712, Masters sailed to England. In London, she applied for a **patent**, a document that stopped people from copying her invention. By law, only men could hold a patent, so Masters got her patent in her husband's name. The patent did explain her role in the invention.

In 1716, Masters applied for a patent for a new fabric, made from weaving the leaves of the palmetto plant with straw. Masters used the material to make hats, which she sold in London.

► Native Americans taught colonists how to grow Indian corn, from which Sybilla Masters's invention made hominy meal. This picture shows a Wampanoag named Squanto showing Pilgrims how to plant corn. Burying fish in the soil helped to fertilize, or feed, the plants.

▼ Native Americans had grown crops such as corn for centuries before Europeans arrived in America. Men did the heavy work of getting the ground ready, but women did the planting and looked after the crops.

◄ These are soldiers in the American Revolution. Benjamin Banneker invented a new way to water the wheat on his farm, so that he could grow more. The wheat helped to feed American soldiers during the war.

▼ The area around Chesapeake Bay, where Banneker had his farm, was good agricultural land.

Benjamin Banneker: The First African American Scientist

Benjamin Banneker was born in Maryland in 1731. His mother was of English **descent**, so Banneker was a free man, not a slave.

In 1753, Benjamin took a pocket watch apart and made drawings of the parts. He carved bigger copies of the parts out of wood and built a clock that worked for more than 30 years.

Banneker started a farm in Maryland, and began to study astronomy. In 1790, **Secretary of State** Thomas Jefferson asked him to help build Washington, D.C., capital of the new United States. When Pierre Charles L'Enfant quit as city **architect**, Banneker redrew from memory the plan for the whole city. From 1791 to 1802, he became well known for publishing a yearly book, called an almanac, about his studies in astronomy. He died in 1806.

Many people in the 1700s believed that black people were not as intelligent as white people. Benjamin Banneker showed that they were wrong.

Thomas Jefferson: Statesman and Inventor

Thomas Jefferson is famous as a politician. He helped to write the **Declaration of Independence** and became the third president of the United States. As were many Americans in the late 1700s, however, Jefferson was also interested in how inventions could make tasks easier.

Jefferson was a farmer. He made a number of different designs for the moldboard, the part of a plow that turned over the earth. Jefferson's designs made it easier for horses to pull plows.

Other inventions grew from Jefferson's work in the government. He had to do a lot of paperwork, so he invented a device that copied letters. He invented a system of codes so that he could send secret messages. Another of Jefferson's inventions, the swivel chair, is still very popular. It is used in many offices today.

► *This drawing shows various kinds of plows used on farms in the 1700s. Jefferson wanted to make a plow that was easier, and quicker, to pull through the soil.*

▲ This portrait of Thomas Jefferson was painted in 1800.

◄ Benjamin Franklin (left) and Samuel Adams (center) helped Jefferson (right) to write the Declaration of Independence in 1776.

▼ Pulling the trigger on this Kentucky long rifle caused the firing pin at the top to fall, striking the explosive charge and firing the shot.

▼ A Conestoga wagon is higher at the back than it is at the front, and has larger rear wheels than front wheels. Such features made the wagon more stable on bumpy ground.

Wagons and Weapons

People who were good with their hands, such as **blacksmiths**, often made small changes to the things that they made. Over time, the changes led to improved versions of the original objects.

Some important improvements concerned traveling. Settlements were often far apart, so people needed wagons to move goods around. There were few roads, and they were muddy and full of holes. In the eighteenth century in Lancaster County, Pennsylvania, German craftsmen began making a new kind of wagon. This was the Conestoga wagon, which was strong and easy to maintain. It became a popular wagon on the American **frontier**.

Rifles were important, both for hunting and for defense. German gunsmiths made Kentucky long rifles, decorated with carving and metalwork. The rifles were easy to load and fire. When America went to war with Britain in 1775, the colonists' weapons were better than those of their enemy.

Remembering America's Early Inventors

The names of many early American inventors have been forgotten. When inventions were the result of small changes made by many people, the inventors' names were often never known. Also, many of the inventions themselves are no longer used, so people are less interested in remembering them.

Another reason American inventors are not remembered is that European science was considered more important than science in the colonies. Europeans did not really take American inventors seriously.

Today, Americans are remembering inventors whose names had been forgotten, such as Sybilla Masters and Benjamin Banneker. In 1980, the Postal Service issued a stamp in Banneker's honor. There are museums about the inventions of more famous inventors, such as Benjamin Franklin and Thomas Jefferson.

Glossary

agriculture (A-grih-kul-cher) The science of farming or raising livestock.

apprentice (uh-PREN-tis) A young person learning a skill or a trade.

architect (AR-kih-tekt) Someone who designs buildings.

astronomy (uh-STRAH-nuh-mee) The study of stars and planets.

blacksmiths (BLAK-smiths) People who make and repair iron objects.

colonies (KAH-luh-neez) New places where people live, but where they are still ruled by their old country's leaders.

compasses (KUM-pus-iz) Devices that indicate direction by using a magnetic needle that points North.

Constitution (kahn-stih-TOO-shun) The basic rules and laws by which the United States is governed.

Declaration of Independence (deh-kluh-RAY-shun UV in-duh-PEN-dints) A paper signed on July 4, 1776, declaring that the American colonies were free from English rule.

descent (dih-SENT) The line of a family from which someone comes.

frontier (frun-TEER) The edge of a settled country, where the wilderness begins.

hominy meal (HOM-nee MEAL) A food ground from kernels of Indian corn.

patent (PA-tint) A document that stops people from stealing an invention.

printing press (PRINT-ing PRES) A machine used to print many copies of something.

secretary of state (SEK-ruh-ter-ee UV STAYT) The person in the government who is in charge of one country's relationship with other countries.

surveying (ser-VAY-ing) The science of measuring land.

Index

A
American
Philosophical
Society, 9, 13

B
Banneker,
Benjamin, 17,
22

E
electricity, 10

F
Franklin,
Benjamin, 9,
10, 13, 22

J
Jefferson,
Thomas, 17,
18, 22

M
Masters, Sybilla,
14, 22

N
Native
Americans, 5

P
patent, 14
Pennsylvania,
13, 21
Philadelphia,
Pennsylvania,
9, 14
plow(s), 6, 18

R
rifles, 21
Rittenhouse,
David, 13

S
surveying, 6, 13

T
telescope(s), 13

V
Virginia, 6

W
wagon(s), 21
Washington,
D.C., 17
water mills, 6
windmills, 6

Primary Sources

Page 4 (top). The engraving of the Pilgrims landing is based on a painting made by Henry A. Bacon in 1877. It shows 15-year-old Mary Chilton, whom some people say was the first person to step foot on Plymouth Rock. **Page 7 (top).** This photograph shows Nantucket Old Mill, which was built in 1746. **Page 7 (bottom).** This engraving of a water mill in Europe was included in the *Encyclopédie* by Denis Diderot, which was published in France between 1751 and 1780. **Page 8 (top left).** *Benjamin Franklin Drawing Electricity from the Sky* was painted by the American artist Benjamin West between 1811 and 1820. In the late 20th century it was used on a stamp commemorating Franklin's 250th anniversary. **Page 11 (top).** This print was made by Currier and Ives in 1876. It shows Benjamin Franklin in a thunderstorm with his son William. **Page 12 (top).** This portrait of David Rittenhouse was drawn by J. Longacre. It was based on a 1796 mezzotint by Edward Savage, which was in turn based on an oil painting made by Charles Willson Peale in 1796. **Page 15 (bottom).** This picture of Native American farmers was created in the seventeenth century by a European colonist. **Page 19 (top right).** The oil painting of Thomas Jefferson is based on a portrait by Rembrandt Peale created in 1800. It is held in the White House Collection of the White House Historical Association. **Page 19 (bottom).** This eighteenth-century engraving shows various kinds of plows used in England in the eighteenth century. Such illustrations were important to spread details of new inventions, because they were very clear drawings. **Page 20 (top).** This is a detail of an original rifle made by a colonial gunsmith in the eighteenth century. **Page 20 (bottom).** This Conestoga wagon is a modern reconstruction of the original wagons.

Web Sites

Due to the changing nature of Internet links, PowerKids Press has developed an online list of Web sites related to the subject of this book. This site is updated regularly. Please use this link to access the list: www.powerkidslinks.com/pselca/iica